Ife ...ographer

wh... ...omes Our

Br... ...*mas* was

c... e Year.

.

...mily,

Wel... they live

Ikenna Goes to Nigeria

In memory of my father, Barrister Nwachukwu Watson Onyefulu
and my mother, Emily, a nurse and stylist – one of the nicest people
in the whole world.

First published in Great Britain and in the USA in 2007 by
Frances Lincoln Children's Books, 4 Torriano Mews,
Torriano Avenue, London NW5 2RZ

First paperback published in Great Britain in 2009
www.franceslincoln.com

British Library Cataloguing in Publication Data available on request

ISBN: 978-1-84507-960-4

Printed in Singapore

1 3 5 7 9 8 6 4 2

Ikenna Goes to Nigeria

Ifeoma Onyefulu

F

FRANCES LINCOLN
CHILDREN'S BOOKS

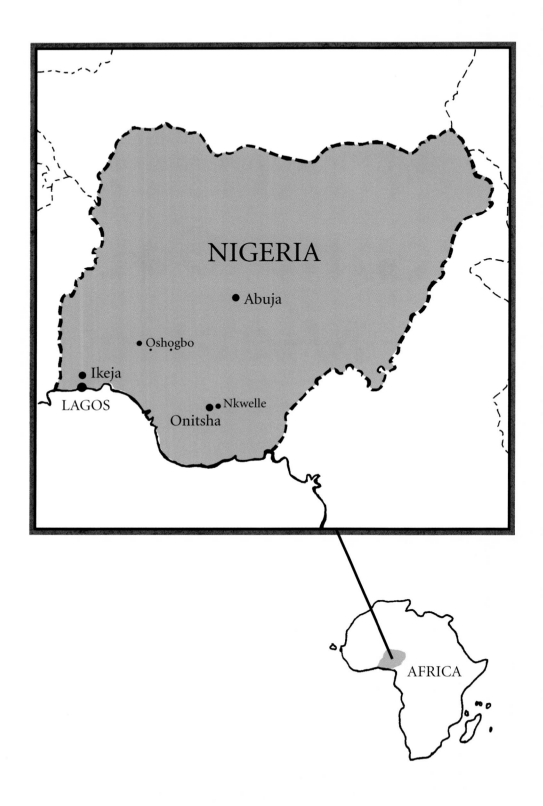

NIGERIA

● Abuja

● Ọshọgbo

● Ikeja

LAGOS

●● Nkwelle

Onitsha

AFRICA

I can't wait to go to Nigeria in July. I have lots of cousins there. I said to my mum, "I bet it will be hot and sunny."

"Not in July, son. It's the rainy season. The rain starts in May and goes on into October."

⌘ Lagos ⌘

Uncle Mazyi came to meet us at the airport in Lagos.

"Welcome to Nigeria, child!" he said.

"Uncle, where are my cousins?" I asked.

"They've gone to school but they'll be back later. We could drive around Lagos for a while," he said.

So we did. We went to Ikoyi, Victoria Island and Ikeya. Uncle Mazyi said a lot of Europeans used to live in Ikoyi, but now rich Nigerians live there.

Great. I'll live in Ikoyi when I'm a rich man.

We went to the Bar Beach in Victoria Island, where I saw some really nice buildings close to the beach.

Uncle Mazyi took a photograph of me sitting on a horse.

Ikeja

Then we went to Ikeja, where I had a lovely swim in the pool.

I met my cousins at last: Somm, Ebuka, Kamsy and Chizitelu, and Aunt Ngo, their mum. I've wanted to meet them for ages.

"Welcome, Ikenna!" they said.

I just wished we'd stayed a bit longer, but my mum and I were going on to Onitsha to visit my other cousins, uncles, aunts and grandparents.

The road to Onitsha

Onitsha, in southern Nigeria, is 650 kilometres from Lagos. It's a long way to drive, but I saw lots of interesting things on the way…

like these signboards by the roadside, which I called "bean-poles",

and a bus with paintings of people sitting in a canoe,

and a hair salon with
a painting of a woman
sitting under a hair-drier…

Then I fell asleep.

When I woke up, we'd
stopped at a market by
the roadside. We got out
and had a look around.
I bought an *ivie* necklace –
it's very special.

Then we drove off and
I fell asleep again.

Onitsha

"Welcome to Onitsha, son!" Mum said, waking me up.
I opened my eyes and saw this long bridge.

We stopped in front of a big house, and my grandmother and grandfather came out.

"Welcome, Ikenna!" they said, and gave me a big hug. It was so nice to meet them!

My grandfather was the first lawyer in his village, and my grandmother was a nurse who had been to Australia to study Ward Management.

I asked my grandmother where my cousins were.

"At school, child," she said, "but they'll be back soon."

"School? But it's holidays now!"

My grandmother laughed. "Not in Nigeria!"

Then she made me some delicious yams with green vegetables for lunch.

When my cousins Chukwudi, Chima and Uche came home, I played football with them.

I wished they didn't have to go
to school next morning. But it
was lovely when Chima and Uche
waved goodbye to me!

It rained and rained and made
lots of puddles.

Nkwelle

Mum and I went to Nkwelle later that morning to visit Great-Uncle Hillary. Nkwelle is a small village about five and a half kilometres from Onitsha. I was happy that it wasn't raining, because I could hear the birds singing in the trees.

My great-uncle was one of the train drivers chosen to take Queen Elizabeth II and the Duke of Edinburgh around when they came to Nigeria in 1956.

Just before we left Nkwelle, he gave me some sweet potatoes, a pineapple and some oranges.

Onitsha

When we got back to Onitsha, my grandmother gave me a pair of shorts she'd made herself. I liked them a lot – they were made from an African print.

I had a special job at Onitsha, feeding the chickens in the mornings and afternoons. It was great!

I was so happy when my cousins started their holidays. I just wish we could have played longer.

✦ Abuja ✦

A week later, Mum and I were off to Abuja, the capital city of Nigeria, to visit Uncle Odili.

Abuja is not as old as Lagos, but I like it a lot.

Meeting Uncle Odili was fun. He told me about a large rock in the middle of a main road just outside the city, called Zuma Rock. I'm glad he took me to see the rock, because people tell a lot of ghost stories about it.

Onitsha

As soon as we arrived back in Onitsha, it was my birthday.
Matthew, who lives with my grandparents, made me
a truck as a present. He made it out of a piece of
cardboard and some glue!

Auntie Debbie organised a family party for me. My first ever party in Nigeria! Everyone was there: my cousins, grandparents, uncles and aunts too.

Auntie Debbie cooked a delicious dish called Jellof Rice just for me.

☒ Ọshọgbo ☒

Then I went to Ọshọgbo in western Nigeria with my mum to see the Osun Festival. The festival is celebrated once a year at the king's palace. We were lucky to be in Nigeria while it was going on.

Mum said it was a chance for women to pray to the goddess Osun to have children or to give thanks for the children they have had.

Mum took a photograph of the goddess.

There were dancers on stilts, chiefs sitting in front row seats, and drummers everywhere.

Suddenly there was a loud bang. It was gunfire – to tell people that the young woman chosen to carry a special calabash to the goddess was ready to leave for the river.

I stood on tiptoe to try to see her, but the woman was covered by heavy cloth, and there were too many people around her. The cloth was to protect the woman on her way to the river.

Onitsha

Then we went back to Onitsha. Now I could play with my cousins again!

Three days later, my mum said, "Ikenna, I want to take a photograph of everybody together, before we go home."

I wish we'd stayed a bit longer. But Mum said we would be coming back next year.

Definitely!

Jellof Rice cooked for Ikenna

Serves 4

You'll need:

- 2 cups rice
- 2 onions
- 3-4 tomatoes
- 4 tablespoons oil
- 4 cups water
- 1 tin tomato purée
- 1 stock cube
- salt
- pinch of red chilli powder
- pieces of chicken (optional)

+ a grown-up on hand to help you.

1. Soak the rice in water.

2. Peel and chop the onions.

3. Heat 3-4 tablespoons of oil in a saucepan and fry the onions until pale gold.

4. Cut the tomatoes into big pieces and add to the saucepan along with the tomato purée.

5. Crumble up the stock cube into the saucepan, then add salt to taste and a little red chilli powder.

6. Add the drained rice, then the water. Cover and cook until the water is absorbed and the rice is cooked - about 10 minutes.

If you are adding chicken, steam the meat first until it is cooked through, then add it at the same time as the rice.

Glossary

Abuja: the capital of Nigeria.

calabash: a container carved out of a large gourd (the hollow, dried shell of a fruit which grows on a type of creeping plant).

Gwari: people living near Abuja who are famous for the beautiful pots they make.

ivie necklace: a beaded necklace traditionally worn by men from Benin.

jellof rice: rice cooked in tomato sauce.

Osun Festival: a festival held by the Yoruba people at Oshogbo once a year to bless childless women and to worship the goddess Osun.

yams: potato-like vegetables growing in the ground, but much bigger and with a different, sweeter taste. Eaten with palm oil they are delicious.

Index

MORE TITLES IN THE
CHILDREN RETURN TO THEIR ROOTS SERIES
FROM FRANCES LINCOLN CHILDREN'S BOOKS

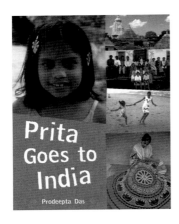

Prita Goes to India
Prodeepta Das

Seven-year-old Prita has come to India for the first time, with her parents and her older sister, to visit their many relatives. She is fascinated by everything, from the Taj Mahal to the village shrines in Orissa; from delicious green coconuts to market stalls filled with savoury snacks; but above all, by the way of life lived by her relatives. Some of it is like her life at home - but much of it is very different.

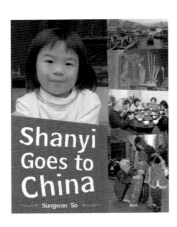

Shanyi Goes to China
Sungwan So

Arriving first on the island of Hong Kong, Shanyi goes by train to Panyu in mainland China to see where her grandmother was born, visits her family's 700-year-old ancestral hall and embarks on a busy schedule of sight-seeing, meeting relations, eating and shopping. From red bean pie to lunar calendars, from firecrackers to dragons, she learns about the Chinese way of life and returns home delighted with the land of her grandparents.

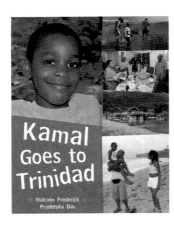

Kamal Goes to Trinidad
Malcolm Frederick
Photographs by Prodeepta Das

"I'm so excited! Today I'm flying to Trinidad and Tobago."
On his first visit to the islands where his parents were born, Kamal learns steelpans and listens to calypso, looks round his father's old school, soaks up the sea and the wildlife – and gets a welcome from his grandparents that he'll never forget.

Frances Lincoln titles are available from all good bookshops.
You can also buy books and find out more about your favourite titles,
authors and illustrators on our website: www.franceslincoln.com